Undoing The Ego Tango

Ego Tango

The ABCs of
Getting More of What You Want
More Often with Less Hassle

by Amy Carroll

THE EGO TANGO
Second edition Green Apple Publishing 2012

First Published Switzerland 2010
by Green Apple Publishing

© Copyright Amy Carroll

ISBN 978-1-4775-4380-1

Printed by Create Space

Cover design by Allyson Ingerman
Interior design and artwork by Kim Molyneaux,
www.kimmolyneaux.com

Predator, Prey or Partner and Invisible Power Game are registered trademarks of SkillsToSuccess. www.skillstosuccess.com

Images:
Little Girl on Phone © Barbara Campbell

Acknowledgements

This was never meant to be a book. Because you are now reading it means there are many people to thank for making it a reality.

To Rebecca Self for her vision and persistence.

To those of you who loaned me your guidance for structuring and your eyes for editing: Pat Kirkland, Mike Carroll, Kevin Carroll, Bob Gignac, Jo Parfitt (a talented and professional editor), Ellen Snortland (a gifted writer, performer and committed activist), Allyson Ingerman for the cover design, and my multi-talented business manager and book designer, Kim Molyneaux, for always finding the perfect picture.

To the many influences that have contributed to the concepts in this book, including the world of improvisational theatre, NVC (non-violent communication), NLP (neuro-linguistic programming), coaching, and Landmark Education.

To my many friends and colleagues who have supported, encouraged, and listened to the multiple stories in and about this book: Robbie Kahn, Karen Tse, Paula Cervoni, Dympna Coleman, Madelon Evers, Elli Von Planta, Danielle Gossett, Naima Meriah, Beth Mazzola, Monica Zumstein, Marlene Granger, Robb and Judith Correll, Gaby Müller, Ann Ambiaux, Zoran Todorovic, Tamara Mosegaard, Stefan Heinz, Lisa Sennhauser, Marie O'Hara, Lynn Denton, Dorna Revie, Kristin Engvig, Rosemarie Germain, Katrina Burrus, Karen McCuster, Ania Jakubowski, Rusty Livock, Christine Perey and many more.

To my clients and coachees for their trust and courage in testing out these techniques and sharing their own successes.

And finally to my entire family and Ghislain for your love, laughter, and unending support.

foreword

by Ellen Snortland

As a writing coach and author, I deal with a lot of writers, their ideas, and the final representation of those ideas—books. Some are good though they're not what I would call evergreen. Folks in the news business use the term *evergreen* to describe articles they have on hand and can run at any time because they are keepers: always fresh, always evergreen.

Amy Carroll's work, and now her book *The Ego Tango*, are evergreen. Why? Because we never stop relating to new characters in this play called life. New people create new challenges. We are always in some sort of dance of communication with people that we live, work, and play with. Amy teaches us to waltz with people instead of tango…unless you choose to tango, which is a legitimate dance after all. The problem is, if you tango as a default and can only do the tango even when the music is a cha-cha, samba, or even a polka, you might be stepping on a lot of toes and listening to the beat of a tune your family, friends, and colleagues can't even hear. You must untangle your feet if your business partner is tap dancing while you are jitterbugging.

You may have noticed that life does not come with an instruction manual. Rather, we depend on life to teach us the lessons we need. But wait! There are some instruction manuals: books like this one that give you templates for re-choreographing your ways of relating.

My particular field of personal safety starts with the absolutely essential and most important tool of self-defense: your voice. I wrote my book *Beauty Bites Beast* because I saw how ill-equipped many people are—especially women and girls—when it comes to saying "no" to unwanted behavior, or to asserting themselves when another human being is crossing their boundaries. You could say that females are often rewarded for Prey behaviors, while males are rewarded for Predator strategies. While that's a gross generality with all sorts of exceptions, Carroll lays out the real challenge of all human beings regardless of gender: how to be a Partner. There are a variety of twists and turns when it comes to partnership, and men certainly encounter rigid gender-based expectations that work against them as potential Partners. They are expected to be aggressive—or in Carroll's model, Predatory—even if they don't naturally behave that way.

Let me give you a specific example about the inspiration *The Ego Tango* has given me in my own life. Our family just had a medical emergency. My cousin "Kitty" and I had to go help "Bunny," another cousin. We all grew up being very close, like sisters. Kitty is very assertive; some might say aggressive. She couldn't understand why Bunny wasn't more vocal and assertive about getting the help she needed. Having just read The Ego Tango, I was able to help Kitty see that Bunny is like a rabbit that gets nervous around Kitty who is like a mountain lion.

We all know that mountain lions consider rabbits a delectable dinner. Bunny would get a glazed look in her eyes and look like she was about to bolt from the room whenever Kitty and I would come around. At a cellular level Bunny was afraid Kitty would eat her!

While we laughed over this analogy, it made sense to Kitty who has since been able to rein in her feline ways enough to offer partnership to Bunny.

There is a Buddhist saying: *When the student is ready, the teacher appears.* The timing on reading *The Ego Tango* was like that. The Predator/Prey distinction prepared me for an emergency and made a difference for all of us. I'm grateful to Amy Carroll for her wisdom.

Learning about partnership has benefits at all levels: personal, family, social, business and international relations. Who can't use more Partners? Carroll teaches us, with entertaining and accessible language, how to take what appears to be discordant music or clumsy dance mates and turn them into graceful colleagues in whatever it is that we want to accomplish. This not only gives us a new understanding and mastery of partnership, it gives us a way to establish a new rhythm for the dance.

With ample anecdotes drawn from all sorts of environments, Ms. Carroll's dancing lessons will have you on the dance floor of life in no time. Wonderful! Fewer broken toes; more music and fun. And if you're in business, there's an added bonus: good partnership will also help the bottom line. Let the dancing begin!

Ellen Snortland
www.snortland.com
Altadena, CA

Contents

Foreword by Ellen Snortland 5

Introduction 11

Key Terms 15

How I Became a Communication Coach
and the Old Lady in My Epiphany 17
    Moment of Truth 24
    Partner Mindset Technique No. 1 –
        Make Up a Different Story 26

Bureaucrats in Action:
Another One Bites the Dust 29
    Partner Mindset Technique No. 2 –
        Make Your Partner Look Good 36
    Moment of Truth 40
    Partner Mindset Tip –
        Stay Calm 41
    Moment of Truth 42

The Whiner and the Wine 45
    Partner Mindset Technique No. 3 –
        Pretend Not to Notice 48
    Partner Mindset Reading Suggestion –
        Emotional Hijacking 50
    Moment of Truth 52

The Key to Household Harmony 55
    Partner Mindset Technique No. 4 –
        The Frame Game 58
    Moment of Truth 60

Booze, Blues and all that Jazz 63
    Partner Mindset Technique No. 5 –
        The Broken Record Approach 68
    Moment of Truth 70

Versailles. Looking for Louis' Throne 73
Partner Mindset Technique No. 6 –
  Stay Detached from the Outcome 76
Key Concepts 78
Moment of Truth 80

Green Suede Jacket 83
Moment of Truth 88

Chivalry in the Station 91
Partner Mindset Technique No. 7 –
  Accept the Offer 94
Moment of Truth 96
Partner Mindset Reading Suggestion – Fun Works 98

Stopped by a Cop 101
Moment of Truth 106
Partner Mindset Reading Suggestion –
  Another Reason to Check your Ego 108
Bonus Partner Mindset Technique –
  Start Every Relationship as if it is Forever! 110

Conclusion: Introducing the Chicken Dance ... 115
Moment of Truth 118
Partner Mindset Reading Suggestion –
  Master Your Mood 122
Partner Mindset Reading Suggestion –
  Leadership Presence 122

About the Author 125

The Ego Tango

The ABCs of Getting More of What You Want More Often with Less Hassle

by Amy Carroll

Introduction

Communicating well can sometimes require a bit of fancy footwork. In any kind of personal or professional interaction, it's easy to get caught up in what I call the Ego Tango, which is triggered by the Invisible Power Game™ (IPG). In almost every exchange one person takes the lead, sometimes a negative one, and others follow, whether they intend to or not. We're usually unaware of the IPG, which causes much of the stress and conflict many of us experience in our communication. We're caught up in the Ego Tango.

Names and locations have been changed to respect privacy.

This book is a learner's guide for identifying and applying the steps to undoing the Ego Tango. When your ego is triggered (you feel disrespected or threatened by someone else), you might naturally respond in either Prey or Predator mode, and you will probably not have a satisfying outcome. This book shows you how to manage your ego to shift the dynamics to Partner, to establish a sense of respect and safety, and to get more of what you want, more often with less hassle.

The following pages are a collection of real life stories I tell in my workshops as a communication coach. Each story illustrates a typical external behavior or an internal mindset I encounter in my work. I teach people how to overcome these blocks so they become more effective and productive in their personal and professional relationships. My hope is that you'll be able to appreciate the humor and humanity in the stories and apply their wisdom to your everyday interactions. You, too, can achieve better results, experience fewer hassles, and have more satisfying relationships.

The ABC Steps to Mastering the Ego Tango

To change any dance from a Prey or Predator interaction to a Partner interaction, you must:

Create **A**wareness — that your ego has been triggered, leaving you feeling either threatened or disrespected.

Identify **B**ehaviors — that will make you more effective.

Finally **C**hange — the dance to experience more collaborative, rewarding relationships.

In each section of *The Ego Tango* you'll find...

A story

A Partner Mindset Technique

A Moment of Truth: things to think about and ways to put into practice each technique

I'm currently creating a companion DVD called
The Ego Tango: Learning the Fancy Footwork.
I will demonstrate the body language that will give you a
clue as to whether you're in a Prey, Predator, or Partner
dance and I will provide tips and tools for getting more of
what you want, more often with less hassle.
For more information, visit: www.CarrollCoaching.com

The Predator, Prey or Partner™ Communication Model

This book would not have been possible without years of research and development by Pat Kirkland, whom I'm lucky to have as my sister. Pat pioneered the Predator, Prey or Partner™ communication model, which is the core of the communication techniques I use in these stories and in my life.

Key Terms

Power: your personal or social power, granted to you by how you show up (how others perceive you). Personal power is separate from positional or hierarchical power, which means anyone can have it, anytime, anywhere!

Predator: a person who appears over-confident, overly competent, or arrogant. A Predator is usually unafraid of conflict and often shows too much respect for self and not enough for others.

Prey: usually a really nice person who will avoid conflict at any cost and who tends to show too much respect for others and not enough for self. A person who is a Prey often takes a subservient or inferior position to others, unintentionally inviting mistreatment from others.

Partner: someone who knows that for communication to be most effective, the power dynamic has to be equal. A Partner does that by showing respect for self and others at the same time.

Invisible Power Game™ (IPG): an unconscious, non-verbal exchange that happens in the first 30 seconds of an interaction, determining who's got the power, who's in control, and most important, how you will be treated.

The Predator, Prey or Partner™ model includes both external behaviors (body language, voice, and words) and an internal mindset. This book deals primarily with the internal mindset. For more information on Pat, the communication model or the Invisible Power Game™, visit www.SkillstoSuccess.com.

This book gives you examples of Predator mishaps, Prey misfortunes, and Partner-in-action stories to demonstrate how you can shift from Predator or Prey into Partner!

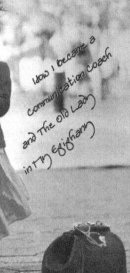

How I became a
communication coach
and The old Lady
in my Epiphany

How I Became a Communication Coach and the Old Lady in My Epiphany

I call this story my epiphany because it includes the moment when I finally realized I had made a significant improvement in my ability to communicate. To explain this, let's back up a bit...

I had been picking fights since about the age of six. It was cute until I turned 15 and started working part time. My first job was at a fabric store, and then I moved to a florist shop. In both cases I had a difficult boss. Not being someone to hold my opinion to myself, I let them know how difficult I thought they were. Picking fights with your boss does not earn you the employee of the month award.

Every new job brought another difficult boss. With each new difficult boss I called my sister Pat and we discussed the situation. Each time she listened with great patience and then said, "Wow, Amy, you have really bad luck!"

Eight jobs, eight difficult bosses and eight sister calls later, I realized that this didn't have anything to do with luck. It was glaringly obvious that I was the common denominator. I was doing something to spark the undesirable behavior and conflict in these working situations. I was perpetuating a predatory pattern of interaction.

I didn't know what I was doing wrong or how to remedy the situation. Deciding to meet the challenge head-on, I read books on interpersonal dynamics, tested out different behaviors and even got therapy (this was long before coaching came along). I worked hard to transform my interaction style. During this time, in 1995, I moved to the Suisse Romande region of Switzerland to fulfill my dream of living in a French-speaking country. And yes, I encountered my share of difficult bosses here as well.

Excited by what I had learned over the previous 10 years, I decided to coach others to shorten their learning curve and reduce the effects of their own communication mishaps. In 2000 I launched Carroll Communication Coaching. (Yes, my business is focused on helping others improve their communication skills; laugh if you must.)

I was putting every effort into building my contacts and circle of influence when a colleague, Judith, invited me to a networking event in the expatriate community. It was exactly the target group I wanted to work with more often. That was when I met Francine.

The event was to kick off at 6 PM with snacks and mingling. Judith said she would arrive at 6:30 PM. "I'll probably get there at 6 PM," I told her, ever the keen bean.

Well, the day of the event rolled around and I was busy multitasking. I decided to finish one more project and arrive at 6:30 PM, the same time as Judith.

As I walked into the room, Judith approached me anxiously. "Amy, where have you been? I thought you were going to be here at 6 PM! I *told* Francine you'd be here at 6 PM! She's been waiting for you!"

"Who's Francine?" I asked curiously, having no idea what the problem was. Judith's hands were balled into fists and her stress level was palpable.

"Francine's this 85-year-old woman who's not very comfortable in social situations, so I told her you'd spend the first half hour with her!"

I didn't hold Judith responsible; she clearly had good intentions. I didn't feel guilty because I couldn't have known of this arrangement.

Judith said, "Well, come on in anyway, I'll introduce you to Francine."

We walked into a room packed with people, and yet it was impossible to miss seeing Francine, a statuesque older woman with a giant beehive hairdo. Two women stood beside her like guards. I approached Francine to introduce myself and held out my hand.

Francine shot me a steely look and spoke sharply. "I have been waiting for you for half an hour! Where have you been?"

My first thought was, *girlfriend... you are messing with the wrong short person!* (I'm 4 ft 10½ in/150 cm on a very good hair day.)

Let me interrupt this scene to explain to you, dear reader, that I have a lively and entertaining imagination. In my mind, I instantly saw my possible options. Luckily, before I opened my mouth, I realized my ego had been triggered. I quickly reviewed my alternatives.

I was tempted to let fly with a Predator response: *Sweetheart, if you haven't gotten your act together by*

the time you're your age, there's nothing I can do for you! (accompanied by a swagger, head tilt, lots of eye rolling and a sarcastic smile).

I'd been verbally attacked in a social situation by a stranger, so some might argue that this response would have been justified. The thing was, I didn't want to be rude to a woman I didn't know. Equally motivating, the English-speaking community in Switzerland is small and I was new in town. I didn't want to alienate them by coming across as nasty in front of the other two women. The last thing I wanted to do was damage my reputation before I'd even built it!

I briefly considered a Prey response. I could go all apologetic and meek. *Francine, I'm really sorry. I didn't mean to keep you waiting. It will never happen again. Please forgive me.* That would be accompanied by lots of anxious movement, skittish eye contact and a bowing head. In addition to my rich imagination, I have an exceptionally strong ego. I can tell you my ego was never going to let me respond like that.

At this point, I was feeling a bit stuck, until suddenly I flashed on a lesson I learned in improvisational theater: **For communication to be effective, the power dynamic has to be equal. The way to equalize the power dynamic is to show respect for yourself and for the other person simultaneously.** In that moment I was able to coach myself. *Keep your body still, hold direct eye contact, put a warm smile on your face and keep your voice calm.*

I did all those things and then without any sarcasm in my voice (which I'm not sure how I managed), I reached out my hand. "Francine, if I had known you were waiting for me, it would have been a pleasure to spend the time with you. It's nice to meet you." I beamed with upbeat and friendly energy.

Francine shook my hand and smiled, melting like an ice cream cone in Texas in August. It was amazing! She was absolutely lovely to me for the rest of the evening.

This was my moment of epiphany. I was tempted to peek up at the skies to see if the clouds had parted and the angels were singing. I realized that by being conscious of the Invisible Power Game™ and putting my ego to one side, I could choose different behaviors over my instinctive reaction and get a very different response. That, for me, really was my moment of awakening to the power I have when I'm aware I can choose different behaviors and change the dance.

It was such a shock to become aware of myself, to see the dynamics at play and to have the ability to instantly shift the status of my relationship. What a huge amount of freedom for all my future interactions with people! Today I use Partner mindset techniques in a wide variety of situations. The level of conflict in my life has reduced dramatically and both my professional life and personal life have benefited significantly.

The important thing to take away is that there is power in *awareness*. That's the first step in changing the dance to a Partner interaction. Start to notice when the Invisible Power Game™ has been set in motion and observe your own reaction to it. Do you become aggressive or defensive towards someone else? Regardless of how anyone else may behave, *you always have the choice of how you respond.*

For now, just begin to pay attention.

Moment of Truth

Here's your first assignment:

Practice becoming aware. Write down the last five or more times you lost your composure and became agitated, anxious or defensive in communication with others.

_____

_____

_____

What were you thinking at the time? How did you feel? How did you notice your ego was triggered?

_____

_____

_____

What happened? What words were used? Be sure to stick with just the facts.

_____

_____

_____

Make Up a Different Story

When someone is behaving in a way that I perceive as negative or disrespectful and it triggers my ego, I practice the technique of making up a different story. I first became aware of this idea in the book *The Dark Side of the Light Chasers* by Debbie Ford, where she talks about making up a different interpretation.

I first applied the Make up a Different Story technique for myself several years ago while driving on the highway from Zurich to Bern. It was early evening when a car flew past me in the left lane. The man was driving so fast and so dangerously that I almost had an accident.

Well, you can imagine some of the choice comments I made about him for the next 20 minutes. After I calmed down a bit, I wondered why he might be driving like that. What could possibly have motivated his behavior? Was he late for an appointment? Did he forget something important back at the office? Did he want to catch the start of his favorite team's final football match? None of the reasons seemed good enough until I thought of this one: his wife must have been having a baby! Yup, that was the excuse that worked for me. That was a good enough reason to explain the reckless driving. I immediately calmed down and had empathy for the guy.

This is the whole point of the technique: to move from feeling angry or defensive toward another person to having empathy and a bit of understanding instead. It probably helped that I once knew a guy whose wife actually did deliver their baby in the car, and yet it doesn't matter whether the explanation is actually true or not. Making up another story helps to calm you down, which is the most important benefit. It encourages you to stay in Partner mode while interacting with the other person.

Another example of this powerful technique comes from Stephen Covey's book *The 7 Habits of Highly Effective People*. Covey tells of a time he was travelling in a subway when a man got on the train with his two sons. The boys were running all over the place bothering other passengers. Covey grew more and more annoyed until finally he asked the father why he didn't do something to control his kids. The father replied, "We just got back from the hospital where their mother died. I don't know how to handle it, and I guess they don't either."

For me, this is a profound example that I can't always know the truth or know why people do the things they do and I may never know 'the truth'. When our assumptions cause us to feel annoyed or defensive toward someone, we can make up a different story. This shifts our internal attitude and allows us to offer empathy and understanding while keeping us in Partner mode. It doesn't matter whether the new story is actually true. The bonus is that this increases the chances of getting a more positive outcome.

TESTIMONIAL

from Tom, a finance manager with a multinational software company

"Last month my colleague sent an email to the entire team stating I had neglected to acknowledge the hard work of two other team members during an end-of-the-quarter presentation. At first I felt angry and defensive, telling myself, 'He's trying to make me look bad.' After a few minutes of ranting, I realized I actually had no clue if that was his intention, so I thought about another story I could make up. With a bit of brainstorming (and a good workout at the gym), I told myself, 'He feels frustrated and jealous about my recent promotion.' This helped me to relax. Later when I talked to him about the email, I was much calmer and we sorted it out in five minutes."

Bureaucrats in Action; Another one bites the Dust

Bureaucrats in Action: Another One Bites the Dust

t was June of 2005. On a balmy Sunday after hiking in the French Alps, I arrived back at my car to discover the window broken and my purse stolen. (Okay, okay. I know I should have hidden it better.) Now, if this has happened to you, you know the whole thing can be upsetting– the damage to the car, the hassle of calling all your credit card companies, let alone losing your favorite lipstick. It can be stressful, to say the least. What I was really worried about was my passport, because I was scheduled to travel to London in just ten days for the start of a huge project with a new client.

I called the US Embassy the next morning. I was in problem-solving mode and asked the man who answered the phone what I needed to do to make my business trip possible.

"No problem. We can issue you a temporary passport," he said. I was so relieved.

"Fabulous," I said. "May I come in on Thursday to collect it?"

"Fine! We'll see you then," he said, and hung up the phone.

Thursday rolled around and I got up early. I arrived at 8:30 AM and was the second person in line; I was most impressed with myself. I waited my turn and then approached the window thinking this was just a matter of paperwork.

I hadn't even finished explaining my situation when the woman behind the bullet-proof glass began scolding me. I'll call her Beverly.

"Somebody could have been using your passport for four days and you're just reporting it now? Why didn't you come in sooner?" Beverly looked at the passport-sized photographs I'd brought. "And those aren't even the right size. You'll have to get new ones."

I was shocked by her response. As calmly as possible, I explained that I'd spoken to a gentleman at the Embassy who told me I could get a temporary passport in time for my business trip the following week to London.

"There aren't any men working here," she said abruptly at the very moment that a man walked behind her desk. It took great restraint not to call this gentleman to her attention. There's one thing I'd like you to keep in mind here, because I sure was: I was still getting my own business up and running. This trip to London was for a major new multinational client. Missing this trip was not an option. It was essential that I receive a temporary passport and time was running out.

Beverly squared her shoulders and looked smug. "And besides, this isn't urgent, you live here, you don't need to get back to the States. The Consul won't approve this." She raised her eyes as if to dismiss me and call forward the next person in line.

My life flashed before my eyes (or maybe it was Beverly's life). I realized I needed to use every communication skill I had ever learned in order to manage myself and get what I needed.

I could have acted like a Prey with whining, crying, and begging. (It might have gotten me what I wanted though would have been humiliating.) I could have acted like a Predator by saying, *Now I know why they make that glass bullet proof!* (This would definitely not have gotten me what I wanted.) Instead I took a deep breath, moved and spoke slowly without a hint of sarcasm, and said, "Do you think you could ask the Consul?"

"No," she snapped. I was running out of options. Whatever I did next, it was imperative that I stayed in Partner mode.

"Do you think you could just check with the Consul?"

She gave me another hostile "No!" and did the eye-raising thing again.

I sat down to fill out the papers she had given me, only to discover I could barely read the writing on the form due to the anger-induced adrenaline pulsing through me. I looked up and noticed a couple sitting across from me with empathic disbelief on their faces. We exchanged a series of non-verbal signals. *Major bummer. What a hassle. Sure hope you have better luck.* This brief bonding moment helped me to lighten up a bit, shake off some of my frustration, and focus on getting back into Partner. I completed the paperwork and concentrated on what was essential: walking out with my temporary passport.

Now I was ready to return the paperwork to Beverly, who was nowhere to be found. After waiting 15 minutes, I went to another window and found the illusive male employee. I approached him hesitantly, sliding the paperwork under the partition. He asked me a few questions, all of which were easy enough to answer, though I still had a strong sense of foreboding.

"Go to the cashier's window and pay for your temporary passport," he said.

I was shocked and ecstatic! Seizing the opportunity before it vanished, I moved quickly to the cashier's window, hoping Beverly would not appear to intercede in my great fortune... only to discover her behind the window!

Beverley squared her shoulders again. "What did you tell the Consul?" she asked through clenched teeth.

I calmly explained that I answered his questions and he told me to come over here and pay.

"Well, I talked to him and we decided to make an exception." Unbelievable. Now she wanted to take the credit!

With all the good will and playfulness I could muster, I said, "Oh, Beverly, thank you so much! I could hug you!" We laughed together and she took my money.

Then Beverly said, "Oh, and by the way, we can use those photos you have with you today for the temporary passport. Here's an envelope with a stamp already on it, addressed to me. You can just mail the photos when you get them taken. And here's a map of where to find the right type of photo machine at the train station." She gave me a wide smile. I had truly won her over.

Amazed and surprised by this dramatic shift in Beverley's behavior, I decided to see just how far I could go. "Could you tell me how to get to the Paraguayan Embassy?" Beverly agreed enthusiastically. She provided the address and a map highlighting which tram I could take to get there. Beverly had transformed from Nasty Predator to Playful Partner.

Two weeks later when I mailed my photos to her, I put in a short, friendly handwritten thank you note.

A month later when I realized the Paraguayan Embassy would not issue a visa in a temporary passport, what did I do? I called my buddy Beverly!

In a friendly, upbeat manner, I explained the situation and asked if I could fax her my residence permit to get my permanent passport processed immediately.

"Sorry, I can only accept faxes from official offices," Beverly said. "You'll have to go to the Consulate near you. Here's the phone number, talk to my colleague Jonas. He will help you."

I made a couple of phone calls and realized there was no way I'd be able to get to the Consulate in time that day. So I called my new best friend back! Hard to believe, isn't it? I explained that it would take me almost two hours to get there and then I paused. The pausing is important. Practice pausing. Create a little room for partnership and step back to see if people will step into that position.

"Hmmmm, two hours..." Beverly said. "Well, why don't you fax it to me then?" The official rule she couldn't change earlier had suddenly become flexible!

Beverly has become a fantastic Partner and resource. She even helps my friends. When one colleague used her services recently, Beverly said, "Hey, if Amy's ever leading a workshop nearby, she should tell me! I'd love to attend."

Make Your Partner Look Good

This concept comes from improvisational theater and is referred to as *having an improv attitude*. It's an essential part of the Partner mindset. This is particularly important when there is potential for conflict and you don't know how to respond. Or more accurately, the response you are considering is not going to improve the situation and may even make things worse. Remember that your Partner is anyone you're interacting with at the moment. It could be a colleague, an airline check-in person, a police officer, or your own Beverly.

Ask yourself, *How can I make my Partner look good right now in this situation?* Just asking the question will start to change your mindset and the response that follows. You could ask a question, offer a genuine compliment, ask for help, or offer a warm smile. In Beverly's case, letting her take credit for getting the job done allowed her to shift into Partner with me. Whatever works!

I often share this example with my students. When I come across a grumpy customer service person at the grocery store, post office, or on the phone and it's toward the end of the day, I ask, "Is it the end of your shift soon?" If the answer is yes, I say, "Well, I wish you a well-deserved, relaxing evening." If the answer

is no, I say, "Well, I hope the rest of your shift is not too stressful." The other person often becomes more energetic and friendly.

Here is an example of a time when I failed miserably by not applying my own advice.

Several years ago I was headed to Paris through the Geneva airport. When flying to France from Geneva, it used to be necessary to go through the French passport control. Accustomed to passport control being in another location, I strolled by the desk without noticing the guard sitting there. In response to my apparent show of disrespect, the guard slammed her hand several times on the desk with great force. In a very sarcastic, hostile manner she said, "Do you need glasses?" Needless to say, I got seriously triggered by her attitude and in my very best French and most sarcastic tone, I shot back a retort. We exchanged several rounds of insults that culminated in the guard insulting my French (which is not particularly difficult to do). I realized that if I continued, I might be invited to spend some time in a small room for an extended period.

The good news was that I made it to Paris on the intended flight; the bad news was my enormous disappointment in my behavior toward the guard. Even though many might think that she had it coming, it's not a shining example of the Partner attitude to which I aspire. I reflected on this incident for several days. It took a while to pull myself out of my feelings of indignation.

Eventually I was able to ask myself, *how could I have made my Partner look good?* I began imagining Partner-like responses to the same scenario. I remembered that after she said, "Do you need glasses?" I had noticed that she was wearing the coolest, most extraordinary glasses. Can you imagine the effect on the guard if I *had smiled and said warmly, "No, and if I did, I would be delighted to have glasses like yours. Those are amazing!"* She probably would have been momentarily perplexed and unable to maintain the same level of aggressiveness towards me. Just a minor shift in her behavior would have felt like an achievement.

When I successfully make my Partner look good (even if I feel less than friendly), it's a victory. I override my instinctual reaction and choose a response that leads to better interactions and desired results.

My recommendation: reflect on interactions of which you may be less than proud. Flex the Partner mindset muscle by brainstorming alternative responses. Enlisting friends may be helpful here. Even though the incident is past, getting your brain to imagine new ways of responding will create a new pathway in your brain and increase your chances of success in the future.

TESTIMONIAL

from Phillip, a product manager with a multinational household products company

"I have a colleague with whom I had never gotten along. Whenever he came by my desk I would say in annoyance, 'What do you want?' Recently I started pretending we are buddies. Now I use an upbeat tone and say, 'How can I help you, Jeff?' It's incredible how much it has changed the way we interact. In fact, I kind of like the guy now. Amazing!"

Moment of Truth

Name some people in your life with whom staying in Partner is sometimes difficult for you (neighbors, colleagues, relatives):

_____

_____

_____

Describe some specific scenarios where you defaulted to a Predator or Prey response:

_____

_____

_____

Imagine alternative Partner responses to the same situations that would make your Partner look good:

_____

_____

_____

Stay Calm

In moments of tension or conflict it's vital that others perceive you as calm. Move and speak slowly. Allow a back-and-forth flow in the conversation. Don't force your point of view. This behavior will most likely diminish the conflict and reduce it to a simple dialogue. You might not actually *feel* calm; that's okay. Your calmness will positively affect the other person, who will begin to calm down and be more willing to listen to your perspective. Calmness increases your chances of being heard and of getting more of what you want.

TESTIMONIAL

from Andreas, head of procurement with a multinational pharmaceutical company

"Last month I was at a customer meeting when a guy came up to me and started yelling about some issue that had nothing to do with me. Instead of trying to calm him down or talk over him in order to explain myself, I simply stood still, kept eye contact, and let him know I was listening. (Actually, I was more interested in getting my heart rate to slow down enough to avoid passing out.) What was surprising to me was how quickly he calmed down and apologized."

Moment of Truth

Think of a situation where you lost your cool. What verbal and non-verbal signals indicated to you (and to others) that you were losing your composure? For example, were you breathing quickly? Did your heart race? Did you speak rapidly or loudly, perhaps interrupting the other person? Did you use a sarcastic or condescending tone with raised eyebrows? If you are not sure, ask someone who has seen you lose your composure. Be sure to ask someone who is not afraid to speak openly to you.

_____

_____

_____

When you notice these signals, what other behaviors can you use instead? For example, you can take slow, deep breaths; relax your face muscles; smile warmly; and nod your head and give other non-verbal cues that you are listening.

_____

_____

_____

TO DO LIST-

- breathe

- smile

- listen

The Whiner and the Wine

On a beautiful, warm September Sunday I headed to a wine tour in Montreux. Now, if there's one thing you learn quickly as a newcomer to Switzerland, it is that the Swiss are always on time! Everything is punctual. This was a walking wine tour that would depart from a tiny wine cellar at precisely twelve noon, snake along the hillside vineyards, and eventually reach a spectacular view and a waiting lunch. If I was not there on time, I would miss the tour, lose my 50 francs, and not have the opportunity to enjoy this wonderful, sunny day out wandering among the hillside vines.

I was running late and already stressed when I hit the post-church traffic. I took the lane I thought would get me to the starting point as quickly as possible. Instead, the road was closed and I was in the wrong lane! I needed to be in the left lane so that I could turn, park my car, and run to the cellar just in time for the tour to begin.

A big, white delivery truck blocked my way. The driver was a bulky man with a bushy moustache and cigarette hanging from his mouth. I had the impression that he wasn't too excited about working on this beautiful Sunday. He had a red light and my lane had a green light. I had to find a solution *fast*. Since his windows were up, I gave him a warm friendly smile and mimed, *Could I turn in front of you?*

Well, apparently I had been spot on about him not having a good day. His mimed response was filled with wildly aggressive and offensive gestures. His flying arms and finger pointing were the equivalent of words I'm sure I don't know in French!

My fantasy response was to channel the former New York driver in me and show him a thing or two! As extremely satisfying as this might have been, I would certainly have missed my wine tour. Conscious that the Invisible Power Game™ was at play, I made a quick decision. Pretending not to notice his behavior, I responded with a bigger smile and mimed, *Oh, great! So it's okay to go in front of you?*

Privately I felt a little stupid.

At first he looked exasperated and frustrated, and then surprised and confused. He just shrugged his shoulders and indicated, *Okay, lady, go ahead of me.*

I felt such a rush of satisfaction for maintaining my composure, not reacting to his aggressive behavior, and getting exactly what I wanted. I practically skipped through the entire wine tour.

Pretend Not to Notice

Fight the urge or 'pretend not to notice'. That is, when the other person is being an idiot, jerk, loser, whatever you want to call it, resist the temptation to react or point this out to them. Pretend not to notice when the other person is being difficult. That is, when they are acting like an idiot, jerk, loser, whatever you want to call it, resist the temptation to react or point this out to them. Instead, continuing to behave like a strong Partner will have a dual benefit. First, if you don't engage, it's difficult for them to continue the fight alone. After a certain point, they realize they are going to look stupid if they continue misbehaving. Second, you help them to save face, which makes it that much easier for them to step into your frame (see Technique 4) and start behaving more respectfully towards you.

Disclaimer: I'm not suggesting you allow yourself to be mistreated by others. If using this technique three to five times has no affect on someone's behavior, address the issue directly at a time you are both calm. I recommend a simple method described by Marshall Rosenberg in his book *Nonviolent Communication: A Language of Life*. Don't let the name intimidate you. I have taught this straightforward method to others for several years with great success.

For me, pretending not to notice is like the martial art of Aikido. Some call it Emotional Aikido. When I can successfully suppress my ego and get a positive outcome, I'm practicing the Partner mindset. Beautifully paraphrasing Italian philosopher Daniel Verde, my brother Kevin says, "Positive Influence is the art of helping others get your way."

Partner Mindset Technique No.3

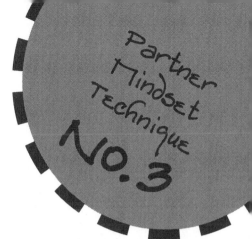

Partner Mindset Technique No. 3

Partner Mindset
Reading Suggestion

Partner Mindset Reading Suggestion

Thinking of Emotional Aikido, I recommend *Hostage at the Table: How Leaders Can Overcome Conflict, Influence Others and Raise Performance* (http://www.hostageatthetable.com). Professor Kohlrieser—an internationally recognized expert on leadership, a professor, and a hostage negotiator—takes the physical reality of being a hostage to the metaphorical level. He shows how living as a psychological hostage is like living with a gun to your head. You are not in the same literal danger as a real hostage, yet you are powerless to act. Any one of us can be held hostage by people, by situations, and by our own emotions. Think back to my example with the French customs officer. That was a classic case of hijacking and I wasn't even on the plane!

Moment of Truth

Who in your life triggers you regularly? It could be colleagues, family members, customer service workers, and so on.

Think of a difficult interaction in which you could have pretended not to notice yet you didn't. What got in your way? For example, did you want to prove you were right? Did you want to let off steam? What else?

What specific actions can you do in those moments to pretend not to notice (such as smile, continue asking questions, keeping upbeat energy, friendly tone)?

You may be concerned that pretending not to notice will make you look incompetent or be mistreated. How is pretending not to notice actually powerful for both parties involved? What are the benefits to you?

_____

_____

_____

With whom might you practice this over the next few days? It could be with someone close to you or a stranger. In the moment, what can you do, specifically?

_____

_____

_____

Notice how this shifts the focus from what the other person is doing to how you're responding. When you begin to manage your own ego, you begin to master these techniques. The results will be surprising!

The key to
Household Harmony

The Key to Household Harmony

Also known as *The Mom and Dad Story*

My amazing and supportive parents, Bud and Claire, have been happily married for over 60 years. Like all couples, they have great moments as well as occasional not-so-pretty moments. I hope they won't disown me for taking artistic license with the following story.

Bud is in the kitchen. Claire is in the living room.

"Claire, where are the car keys?!" says Bud in an annoyed, condescending tone. The unspoken word *idiot* hangs at the end of the sentence. Claire's ego is immediately triggered.

"I don't know, Bud. You had them last!" Claire is pleased because she turned it back on him. In fact, she has one-upped Bud with concrete evidence of his apparent lack of intelligence. Unfortunately, the evening they will now have will not be a Norman Rockwell scene.

The good news is that three of their seven kids are full-time communication coaches. Imagine the same interaction after Claire has received a little free coaching.

"Claire, where are the car keys?!"

Before she reacts to the unspoken message, Claire remembers something one of her very clever children told her. She pauses, takes a deep breath, and responds in a calm, confident, gentle tone.

"I don't know, Bud, let me come help you find them."

Bud is smart. He knows that if he keeps using such a nasty tone, he's going to look stupid. He responds in a more positive, respectful way. "No problem, I'll keep looking. Thanks."

Because Claire chose a different response, Bud's behavior shifted positively.

The Frame Game

As we communicate with each other, human beings construct different frames. Frames are like the mood, tone, and environment or ambience of an interaction. Frames can be positive (friendly, playful, respectful, energizing) or negative (tense, angry, disrespectful, bored). We set frames through our body language, voice, and the words we use.

Unconsciously, we are constantly setting frames and being invited into others' frames. When we're not aware of another person's negative frame, we can get caught in it like a trap.

In the first interaction between my parents, Dad set up a "blame game" frame. Since Mom wasn't aware of it, she reacted defensively, resulting in negative consequences for them both. In the second interaction, Mom was conscious of the negative frame and aware that she had an opportunity to create a more positive frame. She could not force him into the new frame. By making it so appealing (holding respect for both herself and my father), he chose to step in. The result was an enjoyable evening for both of them and their visiting children.

It's important to remember that you can choose whether or not to step into another person's frame. First, be conscious of the frame (awareness). Second, put your ego to the side if you've been triggered and use different behaviors. Third, change the frame to a more positive one and watch the results!

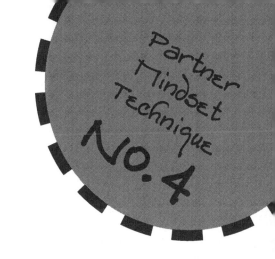

Partner
Mindset
Technique
No.4

Moment of Truth

Whose frames, both positive and negative, do you fall into easily? For example, colleague, partner, neighbor, or check-out clerk.

_____

_____

_____

What kinds of frames, both positive and negative, do you set up in your personal or professional life?

_____

_____

_____

What can you do to set up more powerful partnership frames? What might you have to pretend not to notice?

_____

_____

_____

booze, blues
and all that jazz

Booze, Blues
and all that Jazz

It was July 2005, during the International Montreux Jazz Festival. This giant annual event features hundreds of artisans displaying their jewelry, pottery, scarves and other wares accompanied by magnificent music. It was about 1 AM on a Saturday night. A friend and I were admiring a beautiful display of jewelry; the artist had set out all his rings in neat rows according to size on a long table in his booth.

A rather tall, middle-aged guy staggered over to the display. He drunkenly grabbed a handful of rings. "How much for these?" His words slurred. He leaned against the table with his other hand to steady himself while still holding a half-full wine bottle.

The beautiful arrangement was ruined. The artist didn't seem to know how to handle it, so he tried to ignore the man. My reaction was fierce and immediate: I wanted to toss him to the ground, lecture him on his disrespectful behavior, and then insist that he apologize to the artist. Realizing that this Predator fantasy was likely to end badly, I moved to the other end of the table, as far away from him as possible. Well, I had done such a good job avoiding him that the next thing I knew, I was standing next to his girlfriend! Out of nowhere, with no preparation, no conscious thought, I turned to her using my best French, with a low, gentle, voice I said, "Do you think you could ask him to stop doing that? It's kind of disrespectful to the artist."

She whipped around in a not surprisingly drunken fashion to face her beau. "Honey, this woman wants to say something to you!"

Oh, great, I thought. In a flash I was face-to-face (okay, face-to-chest is more accurate) with the drunk guy. Without missing a beat, I said the same thing to him in the same low, gentle voice. "Do you think you could stop doing that? It's kind of disrespectful to the artist."

"I just wanna get my ear pierced," he bellowed, wavering on his feet.

I wanted to say, *What the hell does that have to do with anything?* Instead, I ignored the subject of ear piercing and repeated calmly and respectfully, "Do you think you could stop doing that? It's kind of disrespectful to the artist."

A few moments later, without commotion or comment, he and his girlfriend turned and staggered away.

Situations like this one often escalate out of control or at least become aggressive and disrespectful. What worked this time? What can we learn from this story?

First I showed respect for him by speaking to him calmly, making eye contact, and using a gentle tone of voice. My words and attitude implied that if he'd known he was being disrespectful to the artist, then of course he would not have behaved like that. It was a way of helping him to save face. (Of course, I had to pretend not to notice and resist pointing out his obnoxious behavior. As satisfying as this may have been, it wasn't going to get me the result I wanted.) What was so amazing was that the message penetrated his drunken state.

The second discovery I made was that, despite my anger towards his behavior, I was able to choose a respectful response that got me what I wanted. My newly developed instinct successfully overrode my ego! My belief is that because I've been practicing these communication techniques frequently in various settings (personal and professional), they have become my new way of being... most of the time.

It's like the analogy of learning a martial art. When you master the art, you develop a new reflex. This story emphasizes the importance of "working out at the gym," so to speak. Practice these techniques and behaviors in short encounters, on a regular basis, so that they become integrated, instinctual and part of your new way of being. It's like upgrading your hard drive (that is, your brain).

These communication skills work with people who are out of control, and they can diffuse a wide variety of tense or difficult situations at home and work. When you are able to use these behaviors automatically in stressful situations, you'll know your practice has paid off!

The Broken Record Approach

Back in the days before iPods, before CDs, before cassette tapes and eight-track tapes, we had records. Records scratched easily. When the record player needle encountered a scratch, the player would get stuck, repeating a fragment over and over. Thus the term *broken record* was born.

While this mindset technique is simple and straightforward, you must be aware in order to apply it. Often when others are upset or angry, perhaps feeling guilty or responsible, they will attempt to pull the conversation off course with distractions. Magicians use smoke and mirrors for the same reason: to divert the audience's attention. The distractions could be unrelated excuses or attempts to turn the responsibility onto you or someone else. Although your ego may be triggered, resist the temptation to discuss side issues or to defend yourself. Instead, keep repeating your request or question in a consistently calm, respectful tone. The eventual result is usually compliance or agreement.

Maintaining the calm tone is extremely important. If you allow frustration or sarcasm to leak out through your tone, it will indicate to the other person that you're hooked. The calm tone shows respect, which makes the other person more willing to comply more quickly. (I'm told this approach is also successful with unreasonable requests from kids and adolescents.)

Partner Mindset Technique No. 5

Moment of Truth

When have you found yourself agreeing to something you hadn't intended? When have you felt confused or manipulated by an outcome?

_____

_____

_____

What appropriate broken record response might you have used?

_____

_____

_____

What are the payoffs when you use the broken record response?

_____

_____

_____

Where is your practice gym? Where are your opportunities to practice at home, work and everywhere in between (for example, after a tough day at work, how can you step into Partner with a sales person in a bad mood, call center worker, cafeteria staff, your kids)?

Versailles. Looking for
Louis' Throne.

Versailles.
Looking for Louis' Throne

f you visit Versailles Palace outside Paris, wear comfortable shoes. It's a big place

I'm glad I did, because this story also involves a little bit of running on my part. I had signed up for a 90-minute tour in the Palace. While I waited for the tour to begin, I wandered around, exploring the gardens. I suddenly realized my tour was to start in five minutes. I sprinted down the garden's beautifully manicured wide avenues and then across a huge courtyard. As I reached the entrance, it occurred to me that I really needed the ladies' room. I was dismayed to realize that the public toilets were back across the courtyard I'd just passed, there were at least 30 women waiting in line, and I'd have to pay. I decided to ask the woman at the reception desk if I could use one of the restrooms in the building where my tour was starting. Now, I knew she was going to say no, so I knew I had nothing to lose. Why not ask?

I consciously stepped into Partner mode as I approached her desk. I made eye contact and smiled. "You wouldn't have a bathroom here I could use, would you?" I kept my energy upbeat while using my very best French.

"Public toilets are across the courtyard," she replied curtly.

I smiled and nodded, maintained eye contact, and held onto my upbeat energy. "Merci, quand même." (Thanks anyway.)

Then magic happened. She spoke as I turned to leave. *"But we can make an exception for you." Holy smoly canoly, Batman*, I thought. She added, "I'm not really supposed to do this."

Using our best Pink Panther no-one-sees-us-doing-this impersonation, we tiptoed across the busy lobby to the private bathroom for employees. "I'm sorry it isn't nicer." Wow, now she was apologizing.

I was thinking, *Hey, sweetheart, I wasn't expecting Louis' throne! Heck it has a door, no line, and I don't have to pay!* I gave her a big smile and a "Merci beaucoup!"

Staying Detached from the Outcome

Let me illustrate this technique by sharing another story with you.

Several years earlier on a trip back to Switzerland from California, I had three suitcases and knew full well that airline regulations would not allow me to check all three without excess baggage fees. I was feeling rather confident (some might call it cocky), assuming that my special communication skills would help me with the check-in agent to avoid having to pay extra fees. I was just starting out in business on my own and had to be a little tight with money. I really didn't want to pay extra charges. That was my downfall; I was attached to the outcome. The whole interaction with the agent was a power struggle. I tried to coerce him "nicely" into making an exception for me; he exercised his discretionary effort (against my requested favor) and said no. That lesson cost me $100.

What I realized from that experience was that I was attached to the outcome and tried to force my way with an unsuccessful result. If you have ever attempted to convince an unwilling toddler to do something, you know what I'm talking about.

While staying detached from the outcome doesn't generally improve the result with a two-year-old, it often improves the result with most people over 4 ft/120 cm. I learned from the baggage experience. I was able to remain detached from what I wanted with the woman in Versailles and as a result, magic happened!

Partner Mindset Technique No. 6

Partner
Mindset
Technique

NO. 6

Key Concepts

Each of us has *discretionary effort* at our disposal.
Imagine a work situation. On average, how much
effort do people put into completing their work?
For most people, it is about 70-80% of their
capacity. This means they have an additional
20-30% of effort available to tap into.

Everyone you interact with has the ability to make
your life easier or more difficult. Imagine a CEO
who rushes past a janitor in the hallway without
acknowledgement. Business as usual. Now imagine
the CEO gives the janitor an upbeat greeting and
calls the janitor by name. The janitor responds with
a friendly "Hello," then adds, "Be careful, the floor
is slippery over there." Now the CEO is more
likely to spend a pleasant weekend with
family instead of at the hospital having
a cast put on.

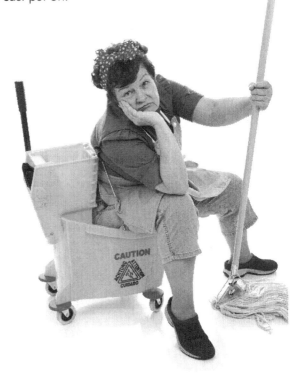

When people feel motivated, they are more willing to tap into that discretionary effort that can make your life easier. By using these Partner mindset techniques, you are helping others to increase their motivation to do that!

In his book *Primal Leadership,* Daniel Goleman describes how humans are hardwired to be affected by each other. Our brain's emotional center, known as the limbic system, is an "open loop" that is susceptible to our interactions with others and directly affects how we feel. Others will be more likely to give you what you want if they feel positively motivated to do so.

The trick here is to remain in Partner mode even when you don't get what you want. Resist showing your frustration by becoming an aggressive Predator or a disappointed Prey. The woman at Versailles let me use the restroom because I continued to treat her with respect, even when she didn't give me what I wanted. Ironically, this made her want to give it to me. So expect seemingly magical outcomes, which will happen with surprising frequency.

Moment of Truth

What is a recent situation with a stranger in which you were attached to the outcome, such as while driving, shopping, in a restaurant, waiting in line at the bank, cinema or airline check-in counter?

....

....

....

How could you have behaved in a more Partner-like way to give the impression of being detached from the outcome?

....

....

....

What happens when you behave this way? How do you benefit from tapping into others' discretionary efforts?

....

....

....

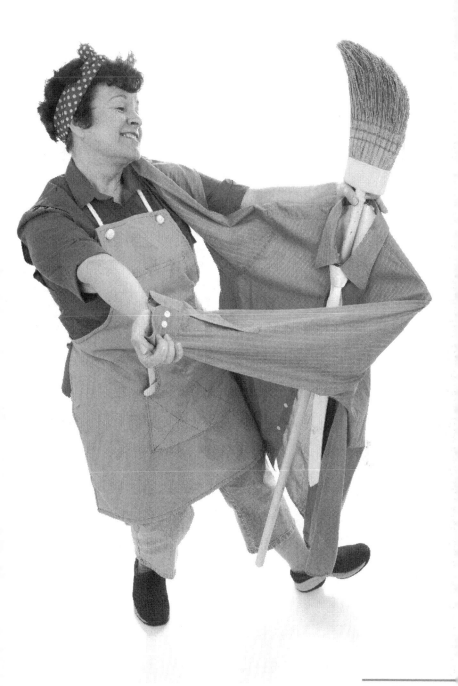

Green Suede Jacket

In case you haven't noticed by now,
I am slightly obsessed with a certain
shade of green...

Green Suede Jacket

This story highlights the following concepts and Partner mindset techniques:

- **Discretionary effort**
- **Staying detached from the outcome**
- **Being the best customer you can be**
- **Stay upbeat and friendly, even when you don't get what you want**

On a cold and dreary day just before Christmas 2006, my sister Pat and I were power walking in a shopping mall in Seattle. Pat and I like to shop, so using the mall to exercise was a slightly dangerous proposition. The pre-Christmas sales were in full swing. As we circled the top floor for the second time, there it was in the window of Coldwater Creek—a green suede jacket. I'm slightly obsessed with a particular shade of green (okay, extremely obsessed) and this jacket was just that color.

I stared at that jacket like some women stare at posters of George Clooney. We ducked into the store. The jacket fitted me perfectly, and the price was reduced by 25%.

I was about to buy it when I noticed that the collar was wrinkled. You can't iron suede. The saleswoman checked for another jacket in the back room without success. She suggested I ask the manager for an additional discount.

At the checkout counter, I explained the situation to the manager and showed her the wrinkled collar. "Would you be willing to give me a further discount? It isn't quite perfect."

"No," she said. "I'm sorry, it's already on sale. I can't discount it any further. Do you still want to buy it?"

I was already in love with my new jacket. "Yes, I'll take it anyway, thanks," I said, sounding not in the least disappointed. I didn't indicate any annoyance with her, though I knew she had the authority (discretionary effort) to grant me a further discount. Instead, as she scanned the price tag and swiped my credit card, we started chatting. I mentioned that I lived in Switzerland.

"Oh, my friend's daughter lived in Switzerland and just loved it!" she said as she folded my beautiful jacket in matching green tissue paper. We were off and rolling in a friendly conversation. Then just before she totalled the sale, she said, "You know the jacket is not quite right... I think I can give you a further discount on it."

Pat started kicking me under the counter as if to say, *This stuff we do really works!*

"Oh! That would be great! Thanks!" I said. Beaming as I got another ten percent off my fabulous green suede jacket, we had a lovely exchange. Pat and I resumed our walk thoroughly pleased with ourselves. I'll bet the adrenaline from the added discount helped me burn a few extra calories!

The saleswoman's reaction occurs when people really feel treated with respect. One of the ways they can tell is that when they don't give you what you want, you're nice to them anyway. They think, *She's still a nice person and not penalizing me. I can give her what she wants, so why not?* This can happen when you stay in Partner and they recognize there are no strings attached.

I have come across two related physiological explanations for why this approach is so effective.

The first, explained earlier, is because people are hardwired to want to help each other (remember the open loop system Daniel Goleman talks about). The second explanation is also connected to the brain. Research by Dr. Gregory S. Berns demonstrated that when we choose a positive response to cooperate with another person instead of an opposing negative response, this behavior activates the joy centers in our brains. We get a hit of pleasure by doing something positive for others. This experience is unofficially known as "our brain on hugs."

So when the manager gave me the discount, she got to feel good about herself for having given me what I wanted!

Moment of Truth

Notice what prevents you from being the best customer you can. What gets in the way for you?

_____

_____

_____

What opportunities do you have to be the best possible customer you can be? (Examples: ask the waiter/waitress' name and use it; if the salesperson looks stressed and you're not in a rush, say you have the time and not to hurry; use an upbeat, friendly, relaxed tone when calling tech support.)

_____

_____

_____

Now practice being the best customer you can be. Select a specific person/situation. What will you do? How will you behave? What will you say?

_____

_____

_____

Bonus Tip

If you are the best customer you can possibly be, you get even more than you thought possible and life will become easier!

chivalry in the station

Chivalry in the Station

In this story I almost missed an opportunity to make someone else look good by not accepting their help.

A few years ago, I was getting off a train in Zurich and was wheeling a suitcase behind me down the aisle towards the door. On this rare occasion, I had almost nothing in my suitcase. It was light as a feather.

A gentleman of about 85 was sitting near the door. He said something to me in German. It's common for the Swiss to look out for others and let them know if they have done, or are about to do, something wrong. So when the gentleman spoke, my thought was, *Aww, man, what did I do wrong now?* I turned around thinking maybe I'd hit someone with my suitcase or run over someone's dog. Not finding anyone in distress, I thought, I *don't know what this guy wants from me.* I said, "Ich spreche kein Deutsch," (I don't speak any German), happy that I had an excuse not to engage further.

Well, another thing to know about the Swiss is that they are seriously gifted linguists. This man heard my accent and said to me in lovely English, "May I help you with your suitcase?" Here I was making up a story that he wanted to tell me I'd done something wrong

and all he wanted to do was help me out!
(*Note to self: remember to apply Partner Technique No. 1: Make up another story – a positive one!*)

My first reaction was to say no. I wasn't going to let an 85 year old man get up to help me with an empty suitcase. Luckily, I realized I was just about to block a cross-cultural, cross-generational offer.

"Oh, that would be lovely," I said.

This man lifted my suitcase, took it from the train, and set it down on the platform. He extended his hand to help me off the train. He flashed a proud smile—chivalry at its best! It was like a scene in a movie from the turn of the century. I was half expecting to see vapor from a steam train as I descended the steps. I don't know who left in a better mood, me or the elderly gentleman! I was happy I'd remembered to accept the offer before it was too late, and I felt the benefits of that simple acceptance for hours afterwards.

Humans are hardwired to want to help others. Selfishly, it makes us feel good when we do good deeds for others.
When you accept an offer from another person, even when you don't really need it, you step into Partner mode. By accepting the offer, you advance the relationship and make your Partner look (and feel) good!

President Woodrow Wilson

Accept the Offer

This story highlights a fundamental principle of improvisational theater: always accept the offer. I've been told the concept was first introduced by Viola Spolin in her book *Improvisation for the Theater*. In order for a scene to move forward, actors accept others' ideas, suggestions, realities, and invitations. If you block (reject) the offer, you are rejecting the other person. In improvisational theater, blocking an offer is the greatest of sins for actors because it can halt or kill a scene. In relationships, blocking the offer can cause communication breakdowns between people.

In the real world, human beings are social animals. We are programmed to work together and depend on each other to get things done. Yet we tend to do a lot of blocking, causing unnecessary stress, frustration, and conflict with others. Some of the reasons we block offers include not realizing an offer has been made; feeling uncomfortable, especially if the offer comes from a stranger; or worrying that with acceptance might be more work. Sometimes it just feels good to say no; it gives a sense of control to say no to someone or something.

Knowing this is such a strong tendency, I regularly practice accepting the offer, whether I'm in public, at work, or with my friends. Kat Koppett, author of *Training to Imagine*, says that accepting the offer is the foundation of all relationships.

Partner
Mindset
Technique
No. 7

TESTIMONIAL

from Alex, finance director with a non-governmental organization

"After my presentation last spring, one of my direct reports approached me and asked if he could give me some tips for improving my speech. I was thinking, 'Are you joking? Who is this kid?' Luckily I caught myself just in time and remembered to accept the offer. I replied, 'Sure, let's talk next week back in the office.' This was a smart move because the delay allowed me time to put my ego in check. It turned out that the kid had some great points on improving both the content and layout. Now he is the unofficial presentations coach for the entire office!"content and layout.

Moment of Truth

Do you block offers before they happen? How?
In all situations, or only some? In which situations
and with whom?

....

....

....

For the next 48 hours, practice accepting every
offer that comes your way, from someone opening
a door, to assistance/advice on a project, to being
offered a seat on the train. An offer can be verbal,
conceptual, physical or emotional. Follow the rule:
never block an offer. (Okay, maybe not everything...)

....

....

....

What kinds of offers did you get? (An offer can
be verbal, conceptual, physical or emotional.)
Examples: someone offered you their seat on a
crowded bus, a smile, someone let you go ahead
of them in line and so on.

....

....

Next, practice extending offers enthusiastically for the next few days. How does it feel when others accept your offers?

_____

_____

_____

How does it feel when they block your offers?

_____

_____

_____

What are some of the rewards and benefits to accepting offers in your life?

_____

_____

_____

Fun Works

Partner Mindset book Reference

Training to Imagine: Practical Improvisational Theatre Techniques to Enhance Creativity, Teamwork, Leadership and Learning by Kat Koppett applies improvisational theater methodologies to developing important business skills. Koppett demonstrates to trainers and managers how they can effectively transfer improv training techniques to their day-to-day business environment.

Even though this book is written for trainers, it also appeals to HR personnel, managers, and team leaders who are interested in increasing their tool kit and enhancing the impact, fun and retention levels of their workshops. No previous experience with improvisation or performing is needed. It offers all the necessary background, and it provides clear and practical instructions with simple and effective exercises. A few years ago my family used it for a party theme for my brother Michael's 50th birthday with great success!

Partner
Mindset
book
Reference

stagged by a cog

Stopped by a Cop

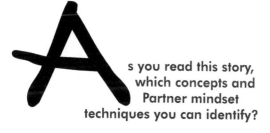

s you read this story, which concepts and Partner mindset techniques you can identify?

It was especially tempting to go Predator or even Prey to get out of the situation I'm about to share with you. This is what happened.

A couple of years ago, I was driving down a road in Vevey, Switzerland, where I now live. I passed a police officer parked perpendicular to me. We were close enough to make eye contact. As I proceeded down the road, a car coming toward me flashed its lights. I realized that I was driving the wrong way down a one-way street with a cop as my eye witness! I took the first turn I could to show the cop I was trying to correct my error. Most unfortunately, I was going down yet another one-way street the wrong way!

I figured I'd better just park the car because this was only going to get worse, and I suspected the cop was close behind. At least it wouldn't look like I was running from anything. About 30 seconds later the cop showed up with sirens blaring.

This guy looked like something out of a Clint Eastwood movie. He sauntered over to my car with his pants tucked into knee-high polished boots. He spoke aggressively in French as if he were scolding a dog. "Do you know what you did? Do you know how dangerous that was?" He held his hands on his hips, making himself even broader.

I had been warned about being stopped by the police in Switzerland. I knew it wasn't like getting pulled over in the United States where you can sometimes laugh and talk nicely to the police officer and get off with just a warning, or even a wave of the hand. Not so, I'd heard, in Switzerland. You get pulled over in Switzerland, you get a ticket.

Still, I knew I had a choice in my attitude. In the 30 seconds before the cop showed up I asked myself, given the fact that I knew I was going to get the ticket, *Amy what do you want to have happen in this situation?* I decided I'd prefer it *not* to be an emotionally painful experience. So I told myself, *just use your best Partner skills.*

Even so, when he reached my car and spoke in such a hostile, disrespectful manner, I momentarily considered my other fantasy choices. I could respond like an annoyed and impatient Predator: *Yeah, yeah, I know, whatever. Alright, just give me the ticket, will you?* The other fantasy response was the semi-pathetic, sobbing Prey who babbles about being a foreigner and female, crying and apologizing for my errors. (Okay, I'm not proud of this, though the Prey response did work particularly well once on a highway in Ohio.)

I resisted both fantasy responses and practiced staying in Partner mode through the way I interacted with him.

"Your documents!" he commanded.

I slowly leaned over to get the paperwork out of the glove compartment. I could feel the nervous energy increasing and did everything I could to control my movements, staying slow and steady. I gave him the papers. I looked him in the eyes.

"Oui, monsieur," I responded to some questions, as calmly as I could.

"Non, monsieur," I responded at the appropriate moments, just as calmly.

I offered no defensive reaction, no explanation. He looked at my driver's license.

"Well, why don't you sign this while you're at it?" he said, handing it back to me. (I'd had the unsigned license eight years by then.) With an unsteady hand, I signed and returned it to him, pretending not to notice the condescending tone of his voice. Then he began to circle the car. I knew he was looking for other violations to add: bald tires, wrong tires for the season, whatever he could find. Swiss cops regularly pull people over for this check alone, and it can be quite costly if they find violations.

The funny part was that I'd had the tires replaced just the day before. I had to fight the temptation to lean out the window and yell, *Yeah, you look at those tires! If you look close enough, you'll see the chalk marks still on them!* Amazingly, I maintained my composure.

He returned to my window and

seemed a little frustrated not to have found anything wrong. So what did he do? He yelled the same thing at me in the same voice, "Do you know what you did!? Do you know how dangerous that was?"

I again resisted the temptation to answer with a sarcastic retort, "Haven't we had this conversation?" Instead, I said simply, "Oui, monsieur. Non, monsieur."

He stood there for a moment. "This would have cost you a lot of money," he said gruffly.

Since this whole conversation was in French, I remember the first thing I did was to translate the past tense of *will*. *Would have.* I thought, *Holy smokes! I'm not getting a ticket!* He handed me back my paperwork and walked away. I sat in my car for several minutes, too shocked to do anything except marvel at what had just happened.

I think what worked in this situation was that I became neither whiny/manipulative nor aggressive/defensive with him. I believe these are the reactions to which police officers are most accustomed. I made a conscious choice to put my ego to the side. I resisted the justifiable temptation to defend myself. When he asked the questions, I communicated respect for both of us. And because I didn't appear to take offense at his aggressiveness, it was as if I didn't give him a good enough reason to issue me a ticket.

What are the concepts and 4 Partner mindset techniques I applied?

Go to my website for the answer CarrollCoaching.com

For me, this is an example of how magic can happen. When you think there is a definite, predictable conclusion, things can change. Even when you're sure of an outcome, magic can happen. When someone is anticipating an aggressive or defensive reaction and instead receives a calm, respectful response, it can be incredibly disarming.

Moment of Truth

When do you say, "Yes, but...!" For example, "Yes, but, I have the right to defend myself in this situation!" Where could you give up the right to defend yourself, or even give up the desire to be right, in order to get a positive outcome? Suppose you miss an important meeting with a colleague and discover that you marked down different dates in your calendars. He implies you got the date wrong. You know for a fact that he got it wrong. In the meeting he was to share some information necessary to complete an important project. Instead of insisting he made the mistake, you choose to reply, "I may have confused the dates. Are you available to speak on Wednesday morning?"

List particular people or situations when it is tempting or even enjoyable to point out how wrong they are:

_____

_____

_____

What could you gain if you give up the need and desire to be right? By taking responsibility in the colleague example, the relationship is undamaged. It's possible that the colleague will also take responsibility for confusing the dates. By preserving the relationship, you get what you want: the much needed knowledge to get the project completed.

_____

_____

_____

How can you respond in Partner ways where you give up the desire to be right?

_____

_____

_____

Another Reason
to Check your Ego

As you can see with these many stories and scenarios, our ego affects our mood, behaviors, and actions. This is just the beginning. If you are ready to advance to the next level of personal awareness and empowerment, I highly recommend Eckhart Tolle's book *A New Earth*. Tolle reveals the mechanics behind the ego that can lead to a shift in consciousness and that can lead to greater inner peace and happiness. If spirituality is not your thing, don't let that get in the way. This book is extraordinary!

Partner Mindset Reading Suggestion

check your

ego

Start Every Relationship as if it is Forever

Luggage Lost in Translation

Last year, my colleague Robbie and I flew economy from Russia to Seattle with an overnight stay in London. Somewhere along the way our suitcases were lost. When we arrived in Seattle, we were seriously jetlagged with no luggage and had to give a workshop. Not a pretty situation. Even worse, this was the third time in a row that Robbie's luggage had been lost with the same airline company! Robbie normally lives and breathes the Partner mindset. This was the last straw for him. I suspected the heat I could feel nearby was fire coming from his ears.

Luckily, Robbie has a very high level of emotional intelligence. By the time we arrived at the lost luggage desk Robbie had cooled off and dragged himself back into Partner mode.

We spent nearly an hour with Rita as she helped with the luggage problem. We had a lovely chat with her. We discovered she was from Romania, and Robbie impressed her with his collection of Romanian words. After the paperwork was finally complete, we asked if there was some

bonus Partner Mindset Technique

compensation for us. She apologized and explained that she could only offer us $75 each since we flew economy. We accepted the compensation enthusiastically, even though I knew it wasn't even going to cover the cost of replacing my makeup! We thanked Rita and said goodbye.

Two days later we got our wayward suitcases. Five days after that, after having checked in online, we were back at the Seattle airport. We stopped by the counter to drop off our luggage and were surprised to see Rita! I mean, seriously, have you ever seen the same airline employee twice? And if it has happened to you, you are traveling way too much!

Rita spotted us, gave an enthusiastic wave, and motioned us to come over.

"I see you received your suitcases. I'm so glad!" she said. Then she peered at us over her glasses with a serious expression. "Please give me your tickets." I was about to explain that we had already checked in when Robbie elbowed me to shut up. Rita disappeared into an office and came back moments later with two seats upgraded to business class!

I believe that bit of magic happened only because we had been incredibly pleasant with Rita during the lengthy paperwork five days prior. The lesson here is to start every relationship as if it is forever. The benefit is twofold; first of all, it counts as going to the gym. The more I practice, the better I get. The second reason to start every relationship as if it is forever is because, well, you never know!

My brother, sister, and I keep a running tab of who gets the most perks from using these techniques, concepts, and attitude. My brother got a free bottle of wine on a flight because he was friendly with the flight attendant. We agreed my business class upgrade on a transatlantic flight trumped his bottle of wine. These techniques pay off in surprising ways. You might want to keep your own list of payoffs. This will help reinforce the power you have to get more of what you want, more often with less hassle.

Conclusion: Introducing the Chicken Dance

The stories in this book illustrate the rewards of applying the Partner mindset in a wide variety of situations. Life keeps getting easier. There's less conflict, less resistance. It can also be extremely entertaining and empowering. I have unbelievable power to influence the people and situations around me, and so do you. I gain multiple benefits, from discounts to upgrades to better relationships. Life is rich.

I'll leave you with a last story from my personal life, because the rewards may be greatest there. While a friend and I were on the beach in Greece a couple of years ago, she told me this powerful story.

A woman named Isabelle had a tense and difficult relationship with her teenaged stepdaughter who visited each summer. One summer Isabelle was especially nervous because the visit was to be extended. She was anxious about how she would manage the tension and avoid the numerous conflicts of the past. For about 10 days Isabelle managed pretty well. Then one night things broke down at the dinner table. Her stepdaughter had been there long enough that the initial welcome, novelty and pleasantries had worn off. Tensions were running high. When her stepdaughter made a derogatory comment about the food, Isabelle felt herself losing her cool. She imagined yelling and throwing broccoli au gratin across the table. Then she suddenly remembered a technique someone had once described: do something completely different and unexpected during moments of stress. Instead of exploding verbally like Isabelle had done in the past, she calmly put down her fork, stood up, pushed back her chair and proclaimed in a booming Master of Ceremonies voice, "It is now time for the Chicken Dance!" Isabelle folded her hands up under her armpits, flapped her makeshift wings, and began squawking loudly, strutting like a chicken on Red Bull across the kitchen floor. The whole family was stunned into silence, and then a moment later they burst into laughter. Isabelle calmly sat down and said with a smile, "Would you pass the broccoli?"

When I heard this story, I immediately described it in an e-mail to my boyfriend back in Switzerland. He had let me know before leaving for Greece that my bursts of anger, when directed his way, weren't working for him. He'd requested that I speak to him more calmly when I get angry. The problem was, my angry reactions felt so difficult to control; I had no idea what else to do. The Chicken Dance offered me an alternative!

I had the opportunity to practice the technique one night not long after that. My boyfriend and I had driven from our home in Vevey to Geneva to attend a Ben Harper concert. The parking lot was packed and we drove around for 20 minutes before we spotted an open space in the next lane over. I was driving, so I asked my boyfriend to hop out and stand in the spot to save it. I drove the car around the long aisle, only to find him standing in front of a car that had just entered our spot!

"What happened?!" I asked with, perhaps, a bit too much energy.

My boyfriend got back in the car and explained that the other driver had aggressively taken the parking spot. I was furious that he had given in and lost our spot so quickly. In a low voice he said, "Honey, is it time for the Chicken Dance?" It clearly was. As soon as I started squawking and flapping my elbows, we were laughing and ended up having a great evening.

The Chicken Dance is a way to shift your mood quickly. It is a powerful technique you can use to alter your behaviors and attitude.

Moment of Truth

And for your last exercise:

When events upset you, what Chicken Dance strategies can you use in personal and professional settings?

Warning: if you risk losing your job by doing the Chicken Dance at work, it may not be appropriate. An alternative idea to the Chicken Dance strategy is to speak gibberish for one or two minutes with a strange accent. (Think outrageous and positive.)

You can use these skills and concepts in every aspect of your life. When you practice bringing awareness to your reactions by employing the behaviors discussed here, you will change the dynamics and reap significant rewards. Use them continuously and you'll get better, faster. Practicing with strangers makes it easier, kind of like having an extra set of wheels when first learning to ride a bicycle. The payoff will be even greater in the relationships that are most important to you.

TESTIMONIAL

from David, a manager at a European telecommunication company

After a week-long intensive leadership training with me, David wrote, "Amy, I've started using what you taught us in the field, especially with people I used to have issues with. I'm already having excellent results. Thank you so very, very much."

During training and coaching sessions, people often ask, "Is it ever appropriate to go Predator or Prey?" This is where these techniques become philosophical. The standard I hold myself to, which I don't always achieve, is this: The only time either response is justifiable is when my life or someone else's life is at risk. That may sound like an unrealistic standard, which is why I'm not always successful at achieving it in the moment. By holding myself to such a high standard, I'm able to remain in Partner mode more and more often.

In fact, my opinion on this philosophy has begun to shift slightly. I was recently hired to give communication training for the

United Nations in Geneva. As a part of the extensive hiring process, I was required to take a four hour online exam. It covered a multitude of scenarios, including what to do if you are ever taken hostage. My first thought was, *I'm doing communication trainings in Geneva is the really an issue?* Then after I reflected a moment I thought, hmm maybe I can learn something here. Sure enough, I did. The recommendation from the UN is that if you are a hostage, never cry, plead or beg for your life.

I analyzed this advice through the Predator, Prey or Partner™ model. They are saying *don't go Prey, even when your life is at risk.* When people are too nice, too submissive or too pathetic, it can actually trigger a Predator response in another person. I now believe that if I were in a life-threatening situation, depending on the circumstances, I would do everything I could to control my emotions and continue to maintain a respectful Partner mindset.

Master Your Mood

Daniel Goleman, who is famous for his work with emotional intelligence, co-authored a book published in 2002 called *Primal Leadership: Realizing the Power of Emotional Intelligence*. I highly recommend it, especially for anyone in a role of leadership, whether in the business world or a social environment. You will discover how the leader's mood has a direct effect on others' attitudes, results and the bottom line.

Leadership Presence: Dramatic Techniques to Reach Out, Motivate and Inspire

Another useful resource is *Leadership Presence: Dramatic Techniques to Reach Out, Motivate and Inspire*. Authors Belle Linda Halpern and Kathy Lubar offer a practical guide for translating acting techniques into leadership presence. The authors show you how to apply qualities to connect authentically in order to motivate and inspire the people you lead while achieving business results.

Partner Mindset Reading Suggestions

Keep in mind: I do not suggest that applying the philosophy and techniques in these stories will eliminate all stress, tension or conflict from your relationships. At the same time, be prepared for magic to happen and discover how you can get more of what you want, more often with less hassle!

A request: please send me your Partner-in-Action mindset stories and successes! I'd be delighted to hear how you've used these techniques and the rewards you've reaped as a result. Send them to me at Amy@CarrollCoaching.com or through my web site: www.CarrollCoaching.com.

Good luck and thanks for reading. Be sure to keep an eye out for advanced lessons and dance steps in *The Ego Tango: Learning the Fancy Footwork* available soon on DVD. For more information, go towww.CarrollCoaching.com and register to receive our newsletter, full of helpful tips and tricks for mastering your Partner Mindset.

About the Author

Amy brings with her over 25 years of personal experience and education. Fourteen of those years were spent working in psychiatric, managed care and educational facilities before becoming a coach, trainer and speaker.

Her understanding of the human psyche is extensive.

About the Author

Amy calls upon her education in psychology, improvisational theater, mediation, and neuro-linguistic programming (NLP) to lead training and coaching programs for multinationals worldwide, working independently and in partnership with SkillsToSuccess Inc, RC Komm S.A., and TNM Coaching.

Amy is a Master Practitioner of NLP, a Professional Certified Coach, member of the International Coach Federation, and has completed the coaching curriculum of CoachU, the foremost coaching institution in the world. She coaches clients to become more dynamic, powerful, and persuasive communicators, developing their ability to influence others by creating powerful partnerships. She does this with the help of the improvisational theatre philosophy to make your partner look good!

Being one of the youngest of seven children taught Amy a lot about communicating for impact! She has coached whole families, MBA students, high-ranking executives, and non-profit leaders around the world. Her extensive client list includes blue chip multinational software and IT companies, world-wide manufacturers of household name brands, international shipping and communications companies, and leading humanitarian organisations.

References

Debbie Ford, 1999, *The Dark Side of the Light Chasers: Reclaiming Your Power, Creativity, Brilliance and Dreams*, New York (NY, USA), Riverhead Trade. http://www.debbieford.com

Stephen Covey, 2004, *The 7 Habits of Highly Effective People,* Bath (UK), Simon & Schuster Ltd. http://www.stephencovey.com

Marshall B. Rosenberg, 2003, *Nonviolent Communication: A Language of Life*, Encinitas (CA, USA), PuddleDancer Press. http://www.cnvc.org/en/about/marshall-rosenberg.html

George Kohlrieser, 2006, *Hostage at the Table: How Leaders Can Overcome Conflict, Influence Others, and Raise Performance*, San Francisco (CA, USA), Jossey-Bass. http://www.hostageatthetable.com

Daniel Goleman, 2006, *Emotional Intelligence: Why it Can Matter More Than IQ*, New York (NY, USA), Bantam Dell. http://www.danielgoleman.info/blog

Daniel Goleman, Richard Boyatzis and Annie Mckee, 2002, *Primal Leadership; Realizing the Power of Emotional Intelligence*, Boston (MA, USA), Harvard Business School Publishing. http://www.danielgoleman.info

Viola Spolin, 1999, *Improvisation for the Theater: A Handbook of Teaching and Directing Techniques,* Northwestern University Press, Reed Business Information, Inc. http://www.spolin.com

Kat Koppett, 2001, *Training to Imagine: Practical Improvisational Theatre Techniques to Enhance Creativity, Teamwork, Leadership and Learning,* Virginia (USA), Stylus Publishing. http://www.koppett.com

Eckhart Tolle, 2006, *A New Earth: Awakening to Your Life's Purpose,* USA, The Penguin Group. http://www.eckharttolle.com

Belle Linda Halpern and Kathy Lubar, 2003, *Leadership Presence: Dramatic Techniques to Reach Out, Motivate and Inspire*, New York (NY, USA), Gotham Books.

Mastering the
Art and Science
of Positive Influence

Carroll Communication Coaching
Rue de l'Union 20
1800 Vevey
Switzerland

+ 41 21 534 7214
+ 41 79 653 5423

Amy@CarrollCoaching.com

www.CarrollCoaching.com

31223889R00073

Made in the USA
Middletown, DE
23 April 2016